West Country
Edited by Angela Fairbrace

Young**Writers**

First published in Great Britain in 2007 by:
Young Writers
Remus House
Coltsfoot Drive
Peterborough
PE2 9JX
Telephone: 01733 890066
Website: www.youngwriters.co.uk

SB ISBN 978-1 84602 926 4

Foreword

Young Writers was established in 1991 and has been passionately devoted to the promotion of reading and writing in children and young adults ever since. The quest continues today. Young Writers remains as committed to the nurturing of poetic and literary talent as ever.

This year's Young Writers competition has proven as vibrant and dynamic as ever and we are delighted to present a showcase of the best poetry from across the UK and in some cases overseas. Each poem has been selected from a wealth of *Little Laureates* entries before ultimately being published in this, our sixteenth primary school poetry series.

Once again, we have been supremely impressed by the overall quality of the entries we have received. The imagination, energy and creativity which has gone into each young writer's entry made choosing the poems a challenging and often difficult but ultimately hugely rewarding task - the general high standard of the work submitted ensured this opportunity to bring their poetry to a larger appreciative audience.

We sincerely hope you are pleased with this final collection and that you will enjoy *Little Laureates West Country* for many years to come.

Contents

Carclaze Junior School, St Austell

Kayleigh Amott (11)	69
Beth Holland (11)	69
Amelia Hasell (10)	69
Georgia Edmonds (10)	70
Ella Griffiths (11)	70
Shannon Darby-Jones (10)	70
Lily Burt (10)	71
Jessica Barter (11)	71
Joel Rowbottom (11)	71
Adam Broadbent (10)	72
Chelsie Roberts (11)	72
Tilly Bryant (11)	72
Emily Putnam (11)	73
Alison Payne (11)	73

St Breock Primary School, Wadebridge

Sam Stevenson (10)	74
Jo Temple (9)	74
Tegan Benney (10)	75
India Laing (9)	75
Ella Wall (10)	76
Rhys Jones (8)	76
Toby Tinker (8)	76
Laura Vinton (10)	77
Lauren Dennis (10)	77

St Mark's CE Primary School, Bude

Joseph Williams (11)	77
Ben Pengilly (10)	78
Catalina Gutierrez (8)	78
Holly McLellan (11)	79
Jack Savage (8)	79
Fay Mannix (10)	80
Emelye Davies (11)	80
Kitty Harding (10)	81
Aiden Gill (9)	81
Amy Hands (11)	82
Emma Hands (11)	82
Eleanor Townsend (9)	83
Ciaran Tape (10)	83
Toby Miles (8)	84

Ben Pye (10)   84
Charlotte Whitfield (8)   85
Demie Williams-Green (9)   85
Reuben Farrell (10)   86
Winnie Stubbs (9)   86
William Phipps (10)   87
Charlotte Chapman (10)   87
Marisa Taylor (10)   87
Lucy Perry (10)   88

St Mary's CE School, Truro
Harrison Raymont (10)   88
Leah Richards (9)   88
Emily Parsons (10)   89
James Doyle (10)   89
Nathan Smith (9)   89
Molly Mason (9)   90
Fleur Anderson (9)   90
Aaron Wilton (10)   91
Alex Cotton (9)   91

The Maynard School, Exeter
Megan Watkinson (10)   92

Urchfont CE Primary School, Nr Devizes
Millie Prichard (9)   92
Patrick Lee (7)   93
Charlotte Kinnaird (8)   93
Annabel Lee (8)   94
Martin Coombes (9)   95
Jamie Hall (8)   96
William Everett (8)   96
Amber Holloway (7)   97
Rosemary Vaux Murray (8)   97
Ellie Gibbs (9)   98
Maddy Borrill (8)   99
Thomas Middleton (7)   99
Lorna Frankel (8)   100
Scott Livermore (8)   101
Amber Weyman (7)   101
Thomas Honeychurch (7)   102

Widey Court Primary School, Plymouth
Sarah Horswell (11)   102

The Poems

Whisked Away

Once there was an island,
a deserted island,
a creepy, deserted island,
there was a beach,
a littered beach,
a disgustingly, littered beach,
and on that beach,
there was a path,
a barely noticeable path,
a barely noticeable, stone path,
and down that path was a hut,
a dusty hut,
a dusty, shattered hut,
and in that hut,
there was a table,
and on that table was a radio,
which said, 'Run away from the horrid beast, help . . . help,'
but what horrible beast?

Chloe Woodroffe (10)
Alderbury & West Grimstead Primary School, Salisbury

King Of Snowflakes

The snowflake, distinct from any other,
Its craftmanship is more magnificent
Than any silver brooch.
The golden six-pointed star is more glorious than a king.
But this fascinating flight to the floor,
Ends so quickly, it's gone like a flash.

Sam Chiverton (11)
Alderbury & West Grimstead Primary School, Salisbury

A Lost Island

Once there was an island,
a lost island,
a dusty island,
and on that island,
there was a tree,
a coconut tree,
a broken coconut tree,
and on that tree,
there was a child,
a small child,
the remains of a small child,
there was a path,
a destroyed path,
an old, destroyed path,
and under that path,
there was a skeleton,
a rotten, old skeleton,
a stinky, old skeleton.

Adam Telfer (10)
Alderbury & West Grimstead Primary School, Salisbury

The Beauty Of A Snowflake

Snowflakes are as delicate as a newborn baby's head,
Snowflakes are as fragile as cracked thin glass,
Snowflakes are as beautiful as fairies,
Snowflakes are more perfect than a 100% test.
Snowflakes are as cold as liquid nitrogen in a fridge.
Snowflakes are love.

Robbie Preest (10)
Alderbury & West Grimstead Primary School, Salisbury

The Reflection

Once there was an hotel,
an abandoned hotel,
a smashed, abandoned hotel,
and in that hotel,
there was a door,
a dusty, dusty door,
and through that door
there was a trap door,
a cobwebbed trap door,
and down that trap door,
deep down that trap door
there was a cage,
an iron cage,
a cold, iron cage,
there was a mirror,
a mirror showing me,
but there was something
else behind me . . .

Tabitha Tossell (9)
Alderbury & West Grimstead Primary School, Salisbury

Snowflakes

As beautiful as a Porsche 911 Carrera.
More delicate than glass.
As clear as water.
As cold as liquid nitrogen.
As beautiful as a cold winter's night.
When it hits the ground it's gone without trace.

Callum Batty (11)
Alderbury & West Grimstead Primary School, Salisbury

The Noise

Once there was a castle,
a deserted castle,
an old, deserted castle,
and in that castle
there was a tower,
a dark, high tower,
and in that tower
there were some stairs,
some stone stairs,
some dusty stone stairs,
and at the top of those stairs,
there was a door,
a rotten door,
a small, rotten door,
and behind that door
there was a room,
a large room,
a gloomy, large room,
and in that room
there was a noise,
a banging noise,
a loud, banging noise,
but what was that noise?

Charlotte Collins (10)
Alderbury & West Grimstead Primary School, Salisbury

Drops

A snowflake as beautiful as a dove,
Gliding through the sky,
Floating over mountains of snow,
And dropping little presents of water,
Then it melts, it's gone.

Georgia Thorne (11)
Alderbury & West Grimstead Primary School, Salisbury

The Ship

Once there was a ship,
a lost ship,
a rotten, lost ship,
and in that ship,
there was a deck,
a damaged, broken deck,
and on that deck,
there was a cabin,
a stinky cabin,
a dusty, stinky cabin,
and in that cabin,
there was a treasure chest,
a dented, dirty treasure chest,
and in that treasure chest,
there was a ring,
a sparkling ring,
a polished, sparkling ring,
and in that ring,
there was an ant,
a squished ant,
a bloody, squished ant.

Sophie Smith (10)
Alderbury & West Grimstead Primary School, Salisbury

Fluttering Down

The wonderful six-pointed star
It falls from the sky so far
Not anything can compare
Not even a firework's flare
The beauty of its pure white
It lands its long-haul flight.

Scott Quinn (10)
Alderbury & West Grimstead Primary School, Salisbury

The Ship

Once there was a ship,
a rotten ship,
an old, rotten ship,
and on that ship
there was a deck,
a dark deck,
a smelly, dark deck,
and on that deck,
there was a cabin,
a musty cabin,
a dirty, musty cabin,
and in that cabin
there was a hammock,
an old hammock,
an old, holey hammock,
and in that hammock
there was a skull!
an old skull!
a rotten skull!

Dean Smith (9)
Alderbury & West Grimstead Primary School, Salisbury

Snowflakes

Snowflakes flutter elegantly
Spiralling to the ground
They drift silently, not even a sound
As picturesque as a rose
Waving side to side
Melts as it ends such a miraculous life.

Ben Smigielski (10)
Alderbury & West Grimstead Primary School, Salisbury

The Laser

Once there was a space ship,
an alien space ship,
a gloomy, alien space ship,
and in that space ship
there was a deck,
a dusty deck,
a modern, dusty deck,
and on that deck
there was a control panel,
a rusty control panel,
a grey, rusty control panel,
and on that control panel
there was a button,
a laser button,
a red, laser button,
and that laser
was ready to fire,
was pointing at
the Earth!

Emma Swanston (10)
Alderbury & West Grimstead Primary School, Salisbury

The Lonely Snowflake

The snowflake in all its beauty,
falls to the earth,
like angels spreading the word of winter.
It floats to the occupied floors,
until it touches the world's uneven surface.
It rests silently - death has arrived.

Sam Wareham (11)
Alderbury & West Grimstead Primary School, Salisbury

The Ghostly School

Once there was a village,
a deserted village,
a quiet, deserted village,
and in that village
there was a school,
a dark school,
an uninhabited, dark school,
and in that school
there was a classroom,
a dark classroom,
a cold, dark classroom,
and in that classroom
there was a table,
a dusty table,
a cracked, dusty table,
and on that table
there was a lantern,
a crushed lantern,
a brutally crushed lantern,
and below that table
there was a chest,
a creepy chest,
a menacing, creepy chest,
and in that chest
there was some gold,
some ancient, lost gold.

Rebecca Ingram (9)
Alderbury & West Grimstead Primary School, Salisbury

Falling

A snowflake, like no other,
as delicately formed as petals on a rose,
gracefully floats to the ground,
like a leaf ending its flight
down from a beautiful willow.

Freya Espir (10)
Alderbury & West Grimstead Primary School, Salisbury

Spooky Island

Once there was an island,
a deserted island,
a spooky, deserted island,
and on that island
there was a forest,
a mystical forest,
a dark, mystical forest,
and in that dark, mystical forest
there was a path,
a shattered path,
a never-ending, shattered path,
and at the end of this never-ending, shattered path
there was a cave,
a stony cave,
a damp, stony cave,
and at the end of this damp, stony cave
there was a tunnel,
an infinite tunnel,
an infinite, shadowy tunnel,
and at the end of this infinite, shadowy tunnel
was a body,
a dead body,
a dead, stabbed body,
and next to this dead, stabbed body
was a knife.

Isabella Gardner (9)
Alderbury & West Grimstead Primary School, Salisbury

Snowflakes

A snowflake's like a newborn butterfly,
So fragile, if you touch it,
It will turn into a thousand pieces of glittery water.
As light as a silky, rose petal,
Colourful, like a rainbow of joy.

Gabrielle Hayball (10)
Alderbury & West Grimstead Primary School, Salisbury

The Lost Ship

Once there was a ship,
a lost ship,
a rotten, lost ship,
and on that ship
there was a deck,
an old, dusty deck,
and on that deck
there was a cabin,
a reeking cabin,
a small, reeking cabin,
and in that cabin there was a step,
a thin step,
a dented, thin step,
and down that step
there was a cellar,
a freezing cellar,
a dark, freezing cellar,
and in that cellar
there were footprints,
heavy footprints,
deadly footprints.

Hannah Hutchby (10)
Alderbury & West Grimstead Primary School, Salisbury

The Perfect Present

As perfect and petite as a
Swallow, swooping and swirling
Across a snow-burdened sky.
Slipping slowly, drifting dewdrops
Leaving frosty tears on your nose and eyelashes.
Dynamically dashing downwards.

Gone!

Katie Blood (11)
Alderbury & West Grimstead Primary School, Salisbury

Island

Once there was an island,
a lost island,
an undiscovered, lost island,
and on that island
there was a jungle,
a creature-less jungle,
and in that jungle
there was a cave,
an empty cave,
an empty, lost cave,
and in that cave
there was a chest,
a rotten, old chest,
and in that chest
there was a cockroach,
a slimy cockroach,
a mutated, slimy cockroach,
and under that cockroach
there was treasure,
old treasure,
old, rusty treasure,
and under the treasure
there were bats,
vampire bats,
killer vampire bats.

Jack Mullett (9)
Alderbury & West Grimstead Primary School, Salisbury

Snowflake

Snowflakes, so carefully formed,
like a beautiful feather,
they slowly float to the ground
and melt like an ice cream,
so small, so quiet,
all settle and fade.

Rebecca Angel (11)
Alderbury & West Grimstead Primary School, Salisbury

The Beauty Of A Snowflake

A snowflake, just one is as delicate
as a newborn butterfly, more beautiful than a moonlit river,
as magnificent as a peacock's feather,
nothing is as delicate, nothing,
something special is a snowflake,
but, now it has fallen, no more beauty,
just a pool of water.

Molly Miller (10)
Alderbury & West Grimstead Primary School, Salisbury

Flake Of Beauty

Crafted beautifully, as perfect as the night sky,
Trickle to the ground only to die.
Falls like a frosty feather, floating in a moonlit stream.
It's your most amazing dream,
Unique, each one its own kind.
The beauty will live on in my mind.

Andrew Bridge (10)
Alderbury & West Grimstead Primary School, Salisbury

Frosted Beauty

As beautiful as diamonds forged from fiery lava,
And as delicate as a raindrop in the river Vltava.
They twist and turn on their way to the floor,
And then disappear for evermore.
All that beauty gone, such a shame,
Because never the same one can you see again.

Faz McVey (11)
Alderbury & West Grimstead Primary School, Salisbury

Snowflakes - Winter's Secret Beauty

More beautiful than a golden rose,
gently as a feather fluttering down
from the wintery grey clouds,
it lands on the ice-cold ground.
The journey of a bright, six-pointed star
has now come to an end.

Egill Tumi Arnason (10)
Alderbury & West Grimstead Primary School, Salisbury

The Design Of The Snowflake

The design of the snowflake as elegant
As the butterflies' wings, falling
From the sky as gracefully as a swan
Gliding down a fast-moving river.
The snowflake is as perfect as the rose,
Snowflakes showing the world winter, over and over.

Liam Sharpe
Alderbury & West Grimstead Primary School, Salisbury

The Floating Snowflake

A glass butterfly, as fair as a rose,
is a beautiful charm that winter chose.
As light as a feather, as fine as gold,
they're a lovely star, and so very cold.
They're so distinct in every way
and don't come every other day.

Ewan Walker (10)
Alderbury & West Grimstead Primary School, Salisbury

The Diary's Secret

Once there was a city,
an empty city,
a dark, empty city,
and in that city
there was a road leading out of town,
an old road,
an old, leaf-strewn road,
and along that road
there was a house,
a deserted house,
a dusty, deserted house,
beside that house
there was a forest,
a gloomy forest,
a lonely, gloomy forest,
and in that forest
there was a thicket,
a thicket of brambles,
a murky thicket of brambles,
in that thicket
there was a pond,
an endless pond,
a dark, endless pond,
and in that pond
there was a box,
a wooden box,
a rotten, wooden box,
and in that box
there was a diary,
a torn diary,
a torn, bloodstained diary.

Who will listen?
Who will tell?
Who will dwell on pages
that have not been read for ages?
In here is written everyone in the city's fate,
but now it is forever too late.

Annabel Salisbury (10)
Alderbury & West Grimstead Primary School, Salisbury

The Mine

Once there was a forest,
a dark forest,
a sinister, dark forest,
and in that forest
there was a tree,
a tall tree,
a looming, tall tree,
and under that tree,
there was a bush,
a berry bush,
a rotten, berry bush,
and under that bush
there was a mine,
a stone mine,
a steep stone mine,
and in that mine,
there was a cave,
a creepy cave,
a damp, creepy cave,
and in that cave,
there was a lamp,
a smashed lamp,
a glowing, smashed lamp,
and through that cave,
there was a light,
a green light,
a flickering green light,
and beside that light
there was a sound,
a cackling sound,
a screeching, cackling sound,
and beside that sound,
there was another sound,
a shouting sound,
a distant, shouting sound.

Daniel Trounson (10)
Alderbury & West Grimstead Primary School, Salisbury

The Gloomy Stadium

Once there was a stadium,
a deserted stadium,
a dark, deserted stadium,
and in that stadium
there was a pitch,
a gloomy pitch,
a turfed up pitch,
and near that pitch
there was a tunnel,
a vandalised tunnel,
a damaged, vandalised tunnel,
and down that tunnel
there was a dressing room,
a dirty dressing room,
a ghostly, dirty dressing room,
and in that dressing room
there was a ghost,
a scary ghost,
a ghost who haunts that stadium.

Matthew Dodkins (10)
Alderbury & West Grimstead Primary School, Salisbury

The Lost Ship

Once there was a ship,
a lost ship,
a rotten, lost ship,
and in that ship
there was a cellar,
a rotten cellar,
a rat-filled, rotten cellar,
and in that cellar
there was a wine rack,
a rotten wine rack,
an old, rotten wine rack,
and old, rotten wine rack that was just about to break.

Daniel Cross (10)
Alderbury & West Grimstead Primary School, Salisbury

Young Writers - Little Laureates West Country

The Island

Once there was an island,
a deserted island,
a stormy, deserted island,
and on that island
there was a path,
a dusty path,
a destroyed, dusty path,
and beside that path
there were some footsteps,
some big footsteps,
some sharp, big footsteps,
at the end of the footsteps
there was a man,
a big man,
a ragged, big man,
and on that man
there was a necklace,
a pearl necklace,
a bloody, pearl necklace.

Jordan Fish (9)
Alderbury & West Grimstead Primary School, Salisbury

My Dad

My dad is as sleepy as a hamster.
And he is as bouncy as Tigger.
My dad swims like a frog.
My dad works as hard as a beaver.
I love my dad.

My dad is as strong as a wrestler.
My dad is as playful as a dog.
My dad is as helpful as God.
My dad is as useful as a blackboard.
My dad loves me.

Tom Froggatt (9)
Alderbury & West Grimstead Primary School, Salisbury

On The Island

Once there was an island,
a stormy island,
a blustery, stormy island,
and on that island
there was a hole,
a dark hole,
a gloomy, dark hole,
and in that hole
there was a crate,
a wooden crate,
a rotten, wooden crate,
and in that crate
there was some treasure,
golden treasure,
sparkling, golden treasure,
and underneath that treasure
there were some bones,
some old bones,
some old bones with a skull.

Ellie Humphries (9)
Alderbury & West Grimstead Primary School, Salisbury

My Dad

My dad plays football.
My dad works like a bee.
My dad is as heavy as a brick.
My dad is as fluffy as a pillow.
My dad loves me.

My dad is as cuddly as a pet.
My dad is as tall as a tree.
My dad is as funny as a clown.
My dad works as hard as a dog.
My dad loves me.

My dad plays football.
My dad works hard as a bee.

Edward James (10)
Alderbury & West Grimstead Primary School, Salisbury

My Dad

My dad can run as fast as a cheetah,
And jumps like a cat.
He can sing like a dove.
He can roar like a lion.
I love my dad.

My dad is as strong as an ox,
As brave as a lion,
As soft as cotton wool,
As kind as an owl,
And my dad loves me.

My dad is as hairy as a lion,
He is as loud as an elephant,
He works hard as a beaver,
He is as funny as a clown.
I love my dad.

Tommy Lush (9)
Alderbury & West Grimstead Primary School, Salisbury

The Tomb

Once there was a pyramid,
a steep pyramid,
a dark, steep pyramid,
and in that pyramid
there was a chamber,
an empty chamber,
an abandoned, empty chamber,
and in that chamber
there was a tomb,
a cobwebbed tomb,
a dusty, cobwebbed tomb,
and in that tomb
there was a sarcophagus,
a dirty, dusty sarcophagus.

Zak Barrett (9)
Alderbury & West Grimstead Primary School, Salisbury

The Lost Ship

Once there was a ship,
a lost ship,
a rotten, lost ship,
and on that ship
there was a deck,
a creaky deck,
an eerily creaky deck,
and on that deck
there was a cabin,
a captain's cabin,
an invisible captain's cabin,
and in that cabin
there was a skeleton,
a deadly skeleton,
a green deadly skeleton,
and in that skeleton
there was treasure,
a gold sparkly treasure,
and in that treasure
a life,
a life lost,
a life lost with treasure,
and in that life
there was a pirate,
an angry pirate,
a mean, angry pirate,
and beside that pirate,
there was a sound
of fighting,
pirates fighting.

Maisie Poulton (9)
Alderbury & West Grimstead Primary School, Salisbury

The Ship

Once there was a ship,
a lost ship,
a forgotten, lost ship,
and on that ship
there was a deck,
a wet deck,
a dusty, wet deck,
and on that deck
there was a flag,
a black flag,
a skull and crossbones, black flag,
and near that flag
there was a body,
a dead body,
a dead, half-eaten body,
and under that body
there was a chest,
a rusty chest,
a rusty, old chest,
and in that chest
there was a cockroach,
a mutated cockroach,
a killer, mutated cockroach,
and under that cockroach
there was treasure,
golden treasure,
treasure guarded by the cockroach.

Harry Palmer (10)
Alderbury & West Grimstead Primary School, Salisbury

Empty School

Once there was a village,
a quiet village,
a deserted quiet village,
and in that village
there was a road,
a small, lonely road,
and in that road
there was a school,
a bare school,
a cold, bare school,
and in that school
there was a hall,
a dusty hall,
a dirty, dusty hall,
and in that hall
there was a classroom,
a destroyed classroom,
a shadowy, destroyed classroom,
and in that classroom
there was a desk,
a wrecked desk,
an old wrecked desk
and near that desk
there was a creature,
a horrible creature,
a grey, horrible creature,
and in that creature's hand,
a body,
a dead body,
a limp, dead body.

Alice Scadden (10)
Alderbury & West Grimstead Primary School, Salisbury

Snowflakes

Snowflakes are more beautiful
than a wistful golden eagle,
as gentle as a feather,
as soft as a pillow stuffed with feathers,
more beautiful than a golden lion,
snowflakes shooting in the air like fire.

Dylan Smith (11)
Alderbury & West Grimstead Primary School, Salisbury

A Pharaoh Is Like . . .

A pharaoh can be as mean as a witch and as powerful as a Minotaur,
More mighty than Queen Elizabeth,
More feared than a dragon,
But sometimes as good as gold,
As kind as a butterfly,
And as clever as a cat,
A pharaoh is richer than Tony Blair,
And as sly as a spy.
He is as wicked as an evil sorcerer casting spells,
As loyal as a dog, as cunning as a fox.
A pharaoh is as well dressed as a supermodel.
That's what a pharaoh is like.

Harvey Walton (8)
Box CE (VC) Primary School, Corsham

Tomb Robber

A tomb robber is like a fast cheetah and as quiet.
He has a spade with him all the time,
The spade has a crushing sound.
And the spade is heavy, it's made of metal,
He has it in his hand all the time.
He is disguised so no one can see him.

Luke Rowell (7)
Box CE (VC) Primary School, Corsham

A Wailing Woman

A wailing woman at home is peaceful,
But when she's at a funeral,
She's like a person when their best pet has died.
She sobs like a child that has fallen over,
She slithers like a snake,
She kneels down and sobs like someone praying.
She looks quite red.
She starts snivelling like my brother.
Then she starts crying like she's having a bereavement.

Martha Benedict (8)
Box CE (VC) Primary School, Corsham

A Tomb Robber Is Like . . .

A tomb robber is like a slithering snake
Going as fast as it can into the jungle,
Catching a mouse and very sneaky.
As rich as the Queen.
Disguised as a chameleon.
Their footsteps are as quiet as a mouse,
As bad as an angry dog,
As dangerous as a crocodile
And as vicious as a rhino.

Connor James (9)
Box CE (VC) Primary School, Corsham

The Nile

The Nile is like a slimy snake swimming out of its depth,
It sounds like a wailing cat, begging for its food.
When it moves out to sea it sparkles like a diamond.
It moves like a tiger shark pouncing upon its prey.
The Nile crashes against the slimy rocks like a cheetah bumping
into a tree.
The glittering waves sparkle like diamonds on a whale.

Edward Cross (8)
Box CE (VC) Primary School, Corsham

A Wailing Woman

The cry of a wailing woman is as loud as the crashing of thunder.
Her tears are as salty as seawater.
Her blue dress sparkles like a gleaming sky on a sunny day.
Her sad face looks like it could make everybody cry.
Her eyes gleam like jewels in the sun.
She looks like she is as sad as a mother leaving her child.
Her body flops down like it's too much for her.
Her silky hair is like soft rabbit fur.

Caitlin Murphy (8)
Box CE (VC) Primary School, Corsham

Tomb Robbers

A tomb robber is as sneaky as a robber stealing a purse,
They're as sneaky as a mouse.
They're quiet as a spider catching its prey.
They're like lightning flying through the sky.
They're like ghosts flying into the tomb.
They're as sneaky as a ninja,
They're digging machines.

Jordan Banks (8)
Box CE (VC) Primary School, Corsham

Pharaoh

As strong as a shark bashing a dam.
As tough as a lieutenant holding off a crowd.
As cunning as a fox tracking its prey.
As cruel as a bull when charging at a target.
As quick as a cat chasing its prey.
As loyal as a guard dog following orders.

Callum Smillie (8)
Box CE (VC) Primary School, Corsham

The Nile

When there is a storm the Nile crashes like a car crash.
The Nile can gently ripple like a bird soaring through the sky.
The Nile runs as fast as a cheetah.
Early in the morning it's as fresh as the wind.
Trickling round rocks carefully but still trying to get over them.
The cold water makes your feet as cold as a penguin treading
through ice.
Water from the Nile makes you think of wet paint, dripping off the wall.

Vanessa Williams (9)
Box CE (VC) Primary School, Corsham

The Nile

The Nile moves like a slithering snake,
It sparkles like a jewel in the sun.
It is as silent as a mouse hiding from a cat,
Though when it is noisy it sounds just like a hissing cat.
It is as quick as a squirrel that's just found a nut.
It's as cold as ice, that has just been unfrozen.
When waves are high it is like a cat hunting its prey,
But when gentle is as soft as the breeze.
As fast as a fox, running from a bear.

Olivia Hewes (8)
Box CE (VC) Primary School, Corsham

The Amazing Nile

The Nile is like a swishing snake,
It sounds like there are horses galloping through it.
It is as beautiful as a butterfly,
Ripples like a dolphin that has been diving for hours.
It moves like a dog that has just doggy-paddled through it.
The Nile lays still at night like a tree when there's no wind.
It looks like a rainbow that moves fast.
The Egyptians love it like they love the sun.

Molly Whitmarsh (8)
Box CE (VC) Primary School, Corsham

A Tomb Robber

A tomb robber is like a spy undercover,
It's as sly as a fox,
As rich as a rich man,
A tomb robber is as strong as a bull when it needs to be,
A tomb robber is as colourful as a rainbow,
As quiet as an ice cream melting in the sun,
As brave as a soldier in the war,
Bad as a devil when he takes the goods,
Amazing as a tiger,
As thin as Sellotape,
As tall as an elephant.

Lucy Cotton (9)
Box CE (VC) Primary School, Corsham

The Nile

It trickles upon the slimy rocks
Like a flat fish on the ocean floor,
It sounds like the breeze of the wind,
It looks as clean as air,
It's as cold as winter,
It gleams in the sun like a dazzling block of ice,
It shimmers in the moonlight like a freezing lake,
It moves like a boulder crashing down a mountain,
It sparkles like the sun.

Matthew Roberts (8)
Box CE (VC) Primary School, Corsham

The Nile

The Nile is like a frosty iceberg floating.
It flows like two baby dolphins flowing slowly and calmly.
It tastes like five salty cold chips that are soggy.

Thomas Parsons (9)
Box CE (VC) Primary School, Corsham

The Nile

The Nile is like a hissing snake that slithers down a hill,
like a sink flooding in a bathroom,
as wide as three football pitches,
all lined up in a row,
as cold as the Antarctic Sea,
like a man with too much hair
as the reeds grow along the sides,
like a crocodile snapping at the rocks,
like a crystal glinting in the sun.

Nathalie Gordon (9)
Box CE (VC) Primary School, Corsham

The Nile

The trees waved in their breezing wind.
It sounded like birds tweeting away on the branches.
The water looked like an ice lolly had been melted into the icy water.
The wind blew so delicately.
The water looked like it was freezing like an ice cube.
The trees looked like men had been stacked up together.

Sophia Harrold (8)
Box CE (VC) Primary School, Corsham

Pharaoh

A pharaoh is like a king,
looking at his people.
He carries a whip
like a flexible sword.
He wears a headdress
which is like a hat.

Matthew North (8)
Box CE (VC) Primary School, Corsham

The Nile

The Nile sounds like an elephant stamping.
It is as cold as the South Pole.
It looks like a giant snake.
It shines like the sun.
It is as slow as a tortoise,
A whale splashing its tail.
As pretty as a rainbow fish.
It is as valuable as a diamond.
It shines more than the stars do.
As wide as two houses.

Jonathan Bazley (8)
Box CE (VC) Primary School, Corsham

The Nile

The Nile sways like a dolphin
It moves really quickly and speedily
It smashes against the heavy rocks
It sparkles in the sun and shines in the sea
It sounds like the wind
The Nile is blue and shining on the top
It is so deep and is filled with colourful fish
Like a Nemo fish and a whale, and more.

Edward Bray (8)
Box CE (VC) Primary School, Corsham

The Nile

The Nile is as pretty as a butterfly.
It looks like a winding snake, catching its prey.
It seems like a glass doll in the sun.
The Nile sounds like a hissing snake.
It is as cold as the North Pole.

Eloise Copping (8)
Box CE (VC) Primary School, Corsham

Tomb Robbers

Tomb robbers are like sharks searching for their prey
Then when they find it they do not share
They are as quick as mice hiding from a cat
And as sly as a fox when searching for a meal
They are quick as lightning to break into tombs
They find the jewels like a dog would find a bone
When finished they slip out like a snake.

Luke Roberts (8)
Box CE (VC) Primary School, Corsham

The Nile

The Nile is a slithering snake,
a hissing cat.
It shines like the sun.
When it is high it splashes like a raindrop,
dripping in a puddle.
It rushes down the hill like a wave breaking
in the sea.

Lucy Rowlands (8)
Box CE (VC) Primary School, Corsham

The Wailing Women

The women wore blue like the River Nile that sways side to side.
They cry like poorly children.
They feel like crying as a baby cries for its mum.
They move slowly and sometimes fall to the ground
onto their knees in a pharaoh's ceremony that's died now
and is going to be buried.

Albany Golledge (8)
Box CE (VC) Primary School, Corsham

An Egyptian Afterlife

It is something you need to know before time goes too far,
The afterlife is like a hope you never reach,
Like a dream that is impossible to be true,
A place you have never been to,
A day without your horrid brother or sister,
As big and mighty as a sky-tall tree,
As precious to you as a diamond,
Like a poor child that has clean water,
As normal as a classmate,
As surprising as finding a lot of money,
Like a play that has taken years to develop,
Like the immense joy of a party,
A shower of golden rain,
A bad storm that ends in never-ending sunshine,
As unexpected as a visit to the Queen,
And as wondrous as Heaven itself,
That's what it's like!

Melissa May (8)
Box CE (VC) Primary School, Corsham

Tomb Robbers

Tomb robbers are as sneaky as a baby cockroach
Like a desperate beggar itching to get rich
As dirty as a mud ditch
As silent as a mouse trying to get the cheese off a table
As wise as King Charles II
As determined as the British Army
Like a sneaky thing trying to get in without being seen
As fast as a jet-powered cheetah
As brave as a father buffalo
As lucky as a princess getting given more ponies
As uncareful as a baby making mistakes
As gentle as the great blue whale
As greedy as a spoilt child getting given a palace
As happy as a pig.

Emilie Bolt (9)
Box CE (VC) Primary School, Corsham

Hallowe'en Night

Never go out on Hallowe'en night,
'Cos it will give you a very big fright.
Never go out on Hallowe'en night,
A vampire might give your neck a bite.
Never go out on Hallowe'en night
Because you might . . . fly!

Harry (11) & Theo Barwood (9)
Bridestowe Primary School, Bridestowe

The Forest At Night

A night in the cold, dark forest
Where the wolves were howling
There was a tall tree,
A tree as tall as a tower.
The bark was as big as a dragon's tooth,
The moon was like an animal's eye,
So high up in the sky.
The hedgehog's spikes upon its back
Were just like a piece of glass.
The glow-worms shone like the moon,
And rabbits nibbled the way through
Acorns, smashed to the ground,
Without even making a sound.
Owls hooting like the sound of a car horn,
Twigs looking like the scales of a fish.
The rocks felt smooth like badger's skin.
The wind howled just like a wolf,
Blowing and whistling through the night.
The moon was as bright as a light in the night.

Darcy Arthurs-Yates (7)
Broomhill Junior School, Brislington

The Forest At Night

Twigs are snapping, leaves are crunching everywhere.
There is howling, growling, hooting and squeaking of lots of animals.
The wolves are sly like hunters seeking prey.
The owls hoot like a whistle on a steamship.
Squirrels hunting acorns, whatever next?
Trees swaying, looking like sharks' teeth.
Rabbits and hares digging houses called burrows.
Glow-worms glowing.
The grass is like snakes' tails.
Mice are squeaking.
The moon is bright, like a dragon's eye.
The bark is like dragons' scales.
Pillars of trees.
The lions and lionesses are growling like dogs getting angry.
Spooky roots.
Little voles and moles, butterflies and dragonflies.
Lynxes and colourful parrots called macaws.
Crabs playing.

Saskia Summerfield (8)
Broomhill Junior School, Brislington

The Forest At Night

The trees were as tall as skyscrapers.
The wind was howling and blowing through my hair.
I heard something move, it was a sort of squeaking sound,
Then I noticed that it was a bat!
The moon was like a rabbit's eye, gloomy in the darkness.
An army of little ants came beside me,
The grass swayed like a snake's tail.
The twigs snapped under my feet.
An owl was settling in the hole of a tree.
Acorns fell like conkers.
An owl swooped above my head like a flying saucer.
The branches looked like the claws of a dragon.

Louise Keep (7)
Broomhill Junior School, Brislington

The Forest

In the wood everything was creepy.
I crept on the ground,
It made a scrunch sound.
Suddenly I heard a wailing sound,
I stopped . . . it was only an owl,
Then I heard a bit of bark break,
I looked at it, it broke off.
Suddenly I heard a tiger snoring,
I was quiet for a minute
Then I ran away,
But everywhere I went it was dangerous.
One place was OK, I went there, I was OK.
I liked it so much I gave a bird some biscuit crumbs,
More and more came.
I looked up and saw the light of the moon, it was very light.
Then I ran out of biscuit crumbs,
So the birds flew away.
I walked away slowly.

Ismail Janjua (8)
Broomhill Junior School, Brislington

The Forest At Night

The trees were as big as a tower
The branches were like claws
And the trees were like scary faces
The bark was like a rhino's skin
The grass was like snakes moving fast

The moon shone as brightly as the stars in the sky
Claws like twigs grabbed at me like tiger's teeth
The noise of animals was as loud as people shouting
The leaves crunching like ice cracking
The acorns falling from the trees like snow.

George Beasor (7)
Broomhill Junior School, Brislington

The Forest At Night

The moon was peering at me with its eye like an animal
And the trees had dragon-like skin
The hedgehogs squeaked like they were being hurt
And rocks as big as rhinos
I heard creaking all around me like a tree being nudged
The rocks as grey as a rain cloud
Leaves as pointy as the point of a knife
The grass was as swishy as centipedes.

George Symmons (8)
Broomhill Junior School, Brislington

The Forest At Night

The midnight sky looks like it is swarming with bats.
The trees look as tall as Kilimanjaro.
The grass looks like snakes' tails.
The bark falling off the trees sounds like a door creaking shut.
The moon looks like a raven's eye.
Some parts of the floor look like animal skin.
Acorns fall from the trees like hailstones.

Michael McCarthy (7)
Broomhill Junior School, Brislington

The Forest At Night

The moon had an eye like a giraffe's.
The stars were little rats' eyes.
The sky was like a big elephant.
Beside me there were trees swaying against each other.
I was on the leaves, I heard the crunching just like this, *crunch!*
There were broken sticks everywhere.

Lauren Smith (8)
Broomhill Junior School, Brislington

The Forest At Night

Trees were swaying like they were doing a dance
And glow-worms were glowing as if they were torches in the ground
The trees were as high as the tallest tower
Though mice were squeaking like bikes
Hedgehogs were as prickly as thorns
And the sky was as dark as an empty cup
But if you go to the forest at night
It is as scary as a monster.

Sarah Craddock (7)
Broomhill Junior School, Brislington

The Forest

The forest was dark and scary.
The branches were like claws.
The boy was very, very, very scared.
A tree looked like a dragon's leg.
The floor had fox's skin.
The moon was like an eye.
The sky was navy blue.
The stars looked like they were coming down.
The trees looked like they had a mouth and loads of fangs.

Jack Millard (8)
Broomhill Junior School, Brislington

The Forest

The forest was dark as the sky.
The moon was like one eye.
The trunks were like claws.
The trees were like towers.
The stars looked like starfish.
The stars were going to hit you.

Jordan Hope (8)
Broomhill Junior School, Brislington

The Forest At Night

The trees looked like scary faces.
When I walked the grass was like snakeskin.
I heard owls howling.
I was scared stiff.

There were branches that made a crunching noise, like crisps.
The moon looked like an animal's eye.
I saw bats that looked like leaves falling from the sky.
Acorns fell from the sky like conkers.
There was an army of ants,
They looked like cherries.
I was tired.

Maisy Hanham (7)
Broomhill Junior School, Brislington

The Forest At Night

As I stepped on a twig
It broke like glass.
I heard a mouse squeaking like a horn.
I saw an owl, swooping about like a kite
And then I saw something that was spiky
And it was a hedgehog's back.
It was like pins and thorns.
The trees were as tall as a giraffe's neck.

Maisie Higgs (8)
Broomhill Junior School, Brislington

The Forest

The moon was gloomy
Branches were like claws
Dark sky was a navy blue
The bark on the tree was lumpy
The grass was like snakes, as the wind blew.

Lauren Carley (8)
Broomhill Junior School, Brislington

The Forest At Night

I stepped into a forest.
The moon looked like an animal's eye and stared at me.

I walked forward and stepped into a puddle of mud
Which looked like scales and it was all squelchy,
I almost got stuck, but I heaved and heaved!

Leaves fluttered down, but . . .
They were actually bats! *Argh!*
I picked up something that felt like glue, but it was a glow-worm,
So I put it down and said, 'Oogh!'

Millie McInnes (7)
Broomhill Junior School, Brislington

The Forest At Night

I walked into the forest,
I could hear howling wolves,
I had brought a torch with me,
I could see pulled-out trees
That looked like they were going to eat you
With sharp teeth to chew you up with.

I heard squeaking hedgehogs
Like someone screaming at a low pitch.
Acorns were smashing against the floor
Like someone smashing a plate.

Tommy Matthews (8)
Broomhill Junior School, Brislington

The Forest

Dragons' arms leaping for me, like a monster getting me.
Stars falling out the sky to get me and make me into a star.
Grass swaying like tree branches, scratching me.
The dark, dark sky was gleaming like a ghost, reaching out for me.
The moon shone out like a monster's big eyes.

Samantha Wood (7)
Broomhill Junior School, Brislington

The Spooky Forest

The wood was as dark as the sky.
The grass slithered like a snake hissing.

The gleaming, golden eye twinkled at me.
The trunks of the trees looked like red fiery dragons' legs.

The sky, in the distance, was very misty and dark,
It was spooky too.

When I looked up I could see stars,
They were making me wiggle,
They looked like they were people running.

Lydia Hurse (8)
Broomhill Junior School, Brislington

Anger

Anger is as red as a slapped face.
It sounds like a gun being fired.

It's black like a pool of ink.
It sounds like raindrops falling.

It's dark like the night sky.
It sounds like a rumbling drum.
It's purple like a rotting aubergine.
It sounds like a crying baby.

Georgia Leonard (8)
Broomhill Junior School, Brislington

The Forest

The forest was very spooky,
The moon looked like one eye.
Very spooked grass,
Looking like slithery snakes coming to get you.
Trees grabbing you
And trying to scratch you.

Jaydene Davidson (8)
Broomhill Junior School, Brislington

The Forest At Night

I went into a forest, every step I took
a branch snapped like a piece of glass.
Trees swayed side to side like a snake
trapped in a volcano about to erupt.
I was getting frightened, but I still carried on.

A wolf was howling like the wind,
standing on a stone,
his teeth were like icebergs, glowing the dark.
A badger was tucked up asleep.

The moon was like a giant eyeball from a giant's head.
The trees were like dragon's claws,
some even looked like they had faces on.

Nicole Fitzsimons (8)
Broomhill Junior School, Brislington

The Storm

The storm is as fierce as a tiger,
The storm is a raging monster,
The wind is as loud as a lion's roar,
Together the wind and rain make the storm.
And together they will never give up.

The murky clouds cover the sky,
Like a blanket of dark fog,
The darkness makes it hard to see,
The screaming and shouting of people,
The flashing lights of oil lamps, swaying in the sea.

The storm bangs and crashes,
The boats fighting to get free,
The gloomy sky,
The gloomy sea,
The storm will never die.

Kimberley Gay (11)
Carclaze Junior School, St Austell

The Journey Of The Pebble

The young and lonely pebble
Sitting on the stones
Shivers in the moonlight
And frowns at the sea

The sea is so, so nasty
Getting him really wet
Sitting there as still as frost
Waiting to be free

Shouting and screaming
'Please pick me up
I'm begging on my knees
Pick me up, pick me up
Oh, please, oh please, oh please.'

The great furious fingers of the sea
Grab the poor little pebble
He is as frightened as can be
Pushed down, down by the fists of the tide
Smashed against the rocks

Leaves scars on the poor little pebble
But still as white as can be
Shaped like an egg
Under the blue, blue sea.

Erin Licursi (11)
Carclaze Junior School, St Austell

My Nature Poem

I see baby tadpoles like bubbles bobbing up and down,
The trees are drifting left and right,
Frosty grass crushing under my feet,
The golden sun shining down,
Birds drifting up and down.

Jacob Summerwill (8) & Anton Barnes (7)
Carclaze Junior School, St Austell

The Pebble

As winter passed by,
the snail-shaped pebble lay motionless on a rocky beach.

When summer came around
the waves crashed onto the pebble
like a cat pouncing for a mouse.
The pebble then sailed quietly to another destination.

The pebble came into shore, shivering in the cold.
This pebble had a marble-like pattern on it.

The pebble lay in hope that he would be taken somewhere.
Then the day came, he was picked up,
this was good news for the pebble.

The light now shone on the pebble
and happiness spread through him.
On his journey he saw things he had never seen before.

The pebble was put on a table.
The pebble looked as if it was a marble heart,
looking for love.
This was the end of the pebble's journey.

Kieran Shopland (11)
Carclaze Junior School, St Austell

The Pebble

Silent, the heart touches you,
Feel the round pebble,
Smooth like a gobstopper.
For a friend, the stony heart waits again.

Smooth and round like a turtle shell,
Lonely it stays, just water around.
Quiet as a drop of salt,
The pebble wishes to have a friend once again.

Louise Symons (10)
Carclaze Junior School, St Austell

The Fish-Shaped Rock

The fish-shaped rock
Came from under the sea.
Shiny and glistening
On the beach.

The pebble was thrown
By the furious waves.
The smooth, hard rock
Now lies on the sand.

The fish-shaped rock
Was picked up by a crab
And tossed into the sea.
Silently the pebble
Stays, lying as cold
As ice, waiting to be found.

The waves pick it up
And let it drift away
Screaming for help.
But still lying on
The water with nothing
But silence.

Abbie Corderoy (10)
Carclaze Junior School, St Austell

The Storm

The wind howled like a wolf
On a mountain
Through the ugly night.

The huge waves opening like a gigantic mouth
The sea bashes against the boat like thunder
The wind is a murderous bullet
Rushing through the air.

Daniel Champkins (11)
Carclaze Junior School, St Austell

The Perfect Storm

The storm was as scary as lightning
striking you down.
The storm was as angry as a dragon,
blowing out flames and destroying the world.
The gale force wind was as strong as a giant's fist.
The sea was as furious as a bomb,
about to blow up.

The boat was as weak as a tiny mouse,
and the sea was as hungry as a shark wanting his dinner.
The boat was helpless
and the sea was playing with it like a ball,
and then one gulp and the boat was gone!

The thunder was booming like a heartbeat, but louder.
The lightning was as bright as light,
right in your eye and was a loud as a giant
shouting at the top of his voice.

The storm is now settling, it has just faded away.
That's the perfect storm.

Tayler Albon (11)
Carclaze Junior School, St Austell

My Senses Poem

I like the taste of the fresh
clear, clean air
I like the sound of birds singing
on a branch of a tree
I can see gliding birds
soaring through the open air
I like the feel of a dog's wet, cold nose
I like the smell of sweet
sweet-smelling perfume.

Rebecca Stevens (7) & Jacob
Carclaze Junior School, St Austell

The Ferocious Storm

The rough fifty-foot waves
Are crashing, smashing
Like a tiger catching its prey.
The flashes of lights
And the sound of a lion's roar
Crashing, smashing
The boat goes down, down
Like being eaten by a lion.

The waves are
Crashing, smashing
No one knows
What is going to happen next
Terror, terror is alive once again
Panicking as the boat
Is dragged, pulled down
Into the ferocious sea.

Danielle Johns
Carclaze Junior School, St Austell

The Pebble

The pebble is so delicate.
No one else can find it.
The pebble is trapped within.
Furious waves move him from side to side.

But now it's summer,
So smooth so dry,
He's lying there with no one by.
How can he move?
When is he going to die?

But now you're here,
Safe and sound,
You will be with me,
So now you're mine,
For the rest of your time.

Zoe Husband
Carclaze Junior School, St Austell

The Stormy Night

The storm is ravenous, raging, pouring,
Rushing, gushing, thundering,
Through the night.
A boat heading into a bombshell.
The sea is a raging monster,
Snacking on fishing boats.
Rough and tough as a tiger's roar.
The gale force winds, whooshing, gushing.
The sea is determined to push the old boat under.
Fighting rushing, mountainous waves.
The mad waves push the wreck
Like a tiny kitten playing with a catnip mouse.
Swooping down into the fiery depths of the deep.
Seconds later, swooshing up into the midnight sky,
The sea swallowing tiny boats for dinner.

Candice Stapleton (10)
Carclaze Junior School, St Austell

The Perfect Storm

The storm
Foul and bitter
The unforgiving, killer waves
Swallow the helpless boat.

The storm
Guiding the boat to the ugly
Repulsive monster's mouth
Swirling round and round.

The storm
The waves growl like a dog saying
'Back off'
The waves don't listen
The storm.

Charlotte Neville (11)
Carclaze Junior School, St Austell

The Storm

The sea is a raging monster,
The wind has joined its side.
The sky is watching gloomily
As the storm is passing by.

The sea swallows up ship after ship,
The wind blows more into the trap.
The sky is a pool of darkness
As the storm is passing by.

The sea is a captivator,
The wind has helped it along.
The sky now unleashes the thunder
As the storm is passing by.

The sea fights an endless battle,
The wind strips sailors of sanity.
The sky flashes with anger
As the storm is passing by.

Rebecca Herrington (11)
Carclaze Junior School, St Austell

The Pebble

The pebble is roasting in the sun,
like a baking potato.
Watching the sea creep in
to cool its scorching body.
Shade it longs for,
from the sun.
Loves it when people put
their blankets over,
to shade it from the sun.

Matthew Collings (11)
Carclaze Junior School, St Austell

Winter

Winter is coming, as the air gets cooler.
Animals start getting ready for hibernation.
The trees lose their leaves
And birds puff out their feathers to keep warm.
The ground is stodgy from all the rain,
And squelches under my feet.
When the snow comes, there's a white carpet everywhere,
It's crunchy and cold.
The wind can be cruel as it whistles and blows everything in its path.
The winter sunshine glares brilliantly down on the world,
Creating a beautiful scene.
Winter is fading for a new year.
Going . . .
    Going . . .
        Gone.

Abbie Margetts (9)
Carclaze Junior School, St Austell

The Lost Garden That I Found

There was a lost garden,
That one day I found,
There were flowers and bushes,
And trees all around.

I wandered and wandered,
Feeling glad for myself,
I looked all around me,
To see a little elf!

He tried to hide,
And run away,
He obviously was scared of me
And didn't want me to stay.

Lana Herrington (9)
Carclaze Junior School, St Austell

Weird Wind

There's a weird wind
Like you're being watched
It's either speeding or slowing
The birds.

There's a weird wind
Whoosh, swoosh, it goes
The windy wind cools the breeze.

There's a weird wind
Like a jet or a helicopter
Whoooooosh, trees waving.

There's a weird wind
Hanging in the sky
Pushing the washing off the line.

There's a weird wind.

Glenn Collar
Carclaze Junior School, St Austell

The Storm

Ferocious winds tossed the boat,
Up and down,
Up and down,
Like a tiger pouncing on its prey
All you see was sea, sea, sea.

Helicopters kept looking for the small boat,
But no sign of it
The boat is hidden by
Mountainous waves.
Lonely, lost, forever.

Charlie Moone (10)
Carclaze Junior School, St Austell

This Tiny White And Silver Pebble

This tiny white and silver pebble,
Squeals in the winter's morn,
As cold as an ice cube,
As quiet as a sea-snail,
Just waiting.

Waiting silently,
To be found,
As the angry waves growl like a tiger . . .
Crash!
The waves take this tiny white and silver pebble
Out to the angry sea.

This tiny white and silver pebble,
Is feeling a little better as spring is here,
'Hooray!' the flowers are growing,
But he is still feeling lonely, cold and sad,
The pebble stretches as he turns to the beaming sun.

This tiny white and silver pebble,
Is wedged into the golden sand,
All alone, all alone,
As he screeches in hope,
Slowly, just slowly,
This tiny white and silver pebble,
Yet then he thinks of what he saw,
As his heart skips a beat,
His family, but no,
This pebble is still alone,
Still alone,
With no one at all.

The tiny white and silver pebble,
Wakes up in his tiny home,
As he yawns and stretches,
To find the sun as always,
The sea as always, but . . .

Something not as always,
The pebble seems to have a grin,
There is lots of laughter and people,
The pebble turns to the sea,
To find,
His family,
Now this tiny white and silver pebble
Is safe and sound at last.

Erin Tregonning (11)
Carclaze Junior School, St Austell

The Pebble

Alone in the sandy bay
Dark as the night sky
Cold as an ice cube
Sitting, just sitting
Waiting for someone to pick it up

Alone in the sandy bay
Smooth as the golden sand
Moving into the light blue sea
To stay warm
Swimming, only swimming
Awaiting a home

The day gets colder
What is coming to the pebble?
The pebble gets lifted out of the sea
Shouting, loudly, shouting
'Thank you, thank you, I'm free.'

Jessica Bate (10)
Carclaze Junior School, St Austell

The Storm

The storm threw the waves onto the ship,
The ship deteriorated as it rolled,
Under the waves.
Sea became the bully,
Ship the victim,
Sea's companions,
Thunder and lightning,
Ship's companions,
Its crew,
Nothing compared to Sea.

Darkness,
Devoured ship,
Daylight,
Everything to nothing
But sea, thunder, lightning remained.
The victim, Ship,
Lay at the bottom of the ocean.

Leanne Wells (10)
Carclaze Junior School, St Austell

The Pebble

I have a special pebble.
It's like a chunk of metal.
If you kick it
It might go too high.
You know the pebble cannot fly.
Now it starts its journey,
Over the moon, over the sun,
Now it looks like an overcooked bun.
It cannot shout.
This is the end, my special friend.

Ricki Tyner
Carclaze Junior School, St Austell

The Summer Pebble

Lonely pebble, still as the moon,
As quiet as a mouse,
Shivering in the freezing frost,
Waiting.

Waiting silently,
The beaming sun peeps through curiously,
The peppermint breeze blows soft against the pebble's
Smooth face,
Grinning.

Grinning lazily,
Lying like a pill, the coconuts fall from palm trees,
White stallions calmly gush through the aqua sea,
Dreaming.
Dreaming magically on the golden sand,
Thinking of what a time he had on summer's sandy beach,
Hopefully wondering if the hot summer will come again.

Emily Jane
Carclaze Junior School, St Austell

The Storm Boat

The boat is tossed around like a cat
playing with a ball of string.
The thunder and lightning collide
in the darkness of the night.
Every visible part of the old boat,
drenched in the bitter waters.

The boat shoots
up, up, up, then crashes down,
down to the bottom of the seabed
waking every fish in sight.

Now it's calm once again,
the storm has finished - for now.

Sam Warren (10)
Carclaze Junior School, St Austell

That Storm

Quick as lightning
The sea headed to shore
I can feel the sea spray
On my face.
Trees holding on for dear life
I can smell a fishy smell
Rubbing against my face
The sea is a wolf, trapped in a cage
Looking for a way out.

A poor boat getting tossed
Like it was caught in a hurricane
The sea pulls the boat
Smashing it like it was nothing.

A poor fisherman trapped at sea
Calling for help,
Life or death.
He's got no hope
He gets tossed like a ball in a football match.

That town now - under the sea.

Ben Adams (11)
Carclaze Junior School, St Austell

The Storm

Quick as an eagle,
Catching his prey,
Hanging over us like a flower,
Ripping up houses.

The waves are a turret
Gun firing indiscriminately,
The storm is a monster
Crushing every single ship.

The storm gets weaker,
As it crushes more.

Karl Hazell (10)
Carclaze Junior School, St Austell

The Storm

The storm
Pulling, ripping, tearing.
The relentless storm chewing
The helpless boat.
Shouts, scream, fear.
Banging, crashing, swaying.
It bellows noises
Throughout the ocean.
Rough as a tiger's roar.
The waves gallop like white
Horses, dragging the boat
Into the terrifying
Monsters mouth.

The storm is alive once more.

Rebecca Dombrick (11)
Carclaze Junior School, St Austell

The Storm

The storm is as strong as an ape
Quick as a BMW
And is like ten tanks
Firing in mid-air.

It is two armies smashing
Into each other.
It is a smart boy
And is a brick wall.

The storm is so strong
It can blow up
The whole
World!

Jacob Mitchell (10)
Carclaze Junior School, St Austell

That Pebble

Freezing cold, lonely pebble,
As cold as an ice cube.
Sits on the beach in the winter,
Waiting to be found.
As the sea drags it in,
The pebble screams with fear.

Suddenly the screaming disappears,
That pebble is drowned by the roaring sea.
The whistling wind deafens that pebble,
Throwing it against the rocks.
When the sea has calmed down
That pebble sits on the rock
Staring into space,
As quiet as a mouse.

The wind starts to blow again,
The pebble awakens.
A tidal wave pulls it into the sea.
The pebble gasps for air,
As it drowns in the deep blue sea.

Once the pebble has caught its breath, it lays on the rock again,
Wishing it was summer.
The pebble opened his eyes,
He sees a little girl staring at him,
It is summer!
She picks him up,
She takes him home.
That pebble is safe now!

Carmen Jones (11)
Carclaze Junior School, St Austell

The Storm

'Help!' cried the powerless fisherman.
The waves attacked the small rowing boat like thunderous gunfire,
The old fisherman holding on to the rear of the rusty boat!

The boat was tossed around the sea like it was nothing,
The waves laughed at the fisherman's despair,
And continued the assault, like a bomb.

The fisherman was the hunted not the hunter,
He was walking into his final breaths
As the poor soul drowned in a watery grave.

The storm never forgives or forgets . . .

Sam Damarell (10)
Carclaze Junior School, St Austell

Pebble

The pebble is cooked as he lies
on the stony sand.
Desperate for a touch or even a lick
of the cool, revitalising, refreshing sea.

He sleeps silently in the hot,
scorching sun, making not a peep of noise.
The pebble waits patiently and helplessly
for the panting dog to rush in.

Alex Wright
Carclaze Junior School, St Austell

The Storm

Quick as lightning,
Louder than thunder,
Gasping for breath - the waves
Crash like and elephant's foot.

The wind is an ice cube,
Smacking on the shore,
While the boat rocks, side to side.
As it's barged by the howling wind,
Whistling like a wolf crying to the moon.

People shouting!
Live or die?

Sophie McKay-Annable (11)
Carclaze Junior School, St Austell

The Storm

Bang, crash, the raging waves toss
the small helpless boat,
like a cat playing with a ball.

The whipping waves shake the whole ocean,
waking up every living creature
under the sea.

The waves are determined
to push the poor boat into the monster's mouth.
The waves swallow the helpless boat.

Adam Cassidy
Carclaze Junior School, St Austell

The Storm

Screaming for help,
Waves crash,
Foamy sea shoving,
Boats rolling,
Scared people hesitating,
Life or death.
Mean Sea, slapped Boat,
Hard as steel,
Waiting, Boat is bullied by angry sea,
Lightning strikes, everything silent,
Everything stops.

Zoe Moyle (11)
Carclaze Junior School, St Austell

A Perfect Storm

A perfect storm
As perfect as a tornado
Twirling round and round
Like a spinning top.

A perfect storm
Like a puff of black smoke
Coming out of a chimney
Killing everyone in its path.

Dean Hodge (10)
Carclaze Junior School, St Austell

The Storm

The boat is being tossed and turned
In the rough, stormy sea.
Huge waves lashing and crashing the boat.

Up, up, up and down, down, down,
The boat sways in the black night.
The boat is being swallowed
By the monster's stormy mouth.

The wind is whistling and howling,
Like a wolf crying to the moon.

Kaiya Bertrand (10) & Josh Raven
Carclaze Junior School, St Austell

The Storm

The wind howled like a wolf on a mountain,
Howling through the ugly night.

The huge waves opened like gigantic mouths,
The sea bashed against the boat like thunder.

The wind is a murderous bullet
Rushing through the air.

The wind crushes the boat into rocks,
Like an earthquake.

Jorin Lenz-Williams (11)
Carclaze Junior School, St Austell

The Storm

The sea is an angry lion
Waiting for its prey
An ice-cold, wet
Shudder runs down their backs
The whistling wind bellows
Gigantic waves slap the boat
Rocking it
Ear-splitting noise
A storm is blood-curdling, like a monster
Awaiting your life or death.

Hannah Wyness (11)
Carclaze Junior School, St Austell

Ice Poem

Water and ice, both the same thing,
Water is ice, ice is water,
But ice drip-drip-drips
Water pouring in a cup.
Ice is freezing, water can be cold or hot.
Most people have a freezer and a fridge,
A fridge is not that cold,
A freezer is like the North Pole.
So what do you think? Is it freezing or hot today?

Millie King (9)
Carclaze Junior School, St Austell

Teachers Can . . .

Teachers can talk
Teachers can walk
And teachers can eat pork
Teachers can care
And teachers can share.

Lee Pollard (7)
Exminster Primary School, Exeter

The Everything Poem

Inky pens and clucking hens,
Creaking doors and messy floors,
Messy rooms and witches' brooms,
Yellow, green and the fairy queen,
Orange and blue doesn't suit you,
Cows go moo but babies go *boo hoo,*
Oranges are yummy because they fill my
Tummy!

William Gooding (8)
Exminster Primary School, Exeter

Food

Pineapples; yummy and prickly.
Jellies; tasty and wobbly.
Swede; yucky and squidgy.
Carrots; grow in the ground.
Potatoes; mashy and fluffy.
Sweets; chewy and gooey.
Melons; juicy and hard.
Sausages; you put in a bap.

I like food.

Eleanor Welch (8)
Exminster Primary School, Exeter

An Acrostic Poem

P ink petals
L ovely lime
A pples juicy
N ew flowers
T ickly tiger lillies
S unny sunflowers.

Charlie Jeffs (7)
Exminster Primary School, Exeter

On The Beach

On the beach you find lots of things,
Lovely stones and golden rings!
Up the mountain, through a cave,
Out the end, see a tidal wave!
Down some steps, swim in the sea,
Get so wet and smile with glee.
Dripping, soaked, walking over sand,
Saying that it's very grand.
There's the golden sun above,
Flying like a silver dove.
Pink and pearly lying there,
Straight and twirly shell!

Bethany Lake (7)
Exminster Primary School, Exeter

Teachers Can . . .

Teachers can work
And teachers can walk.
Teachers can teach
And teachers can talk.
Teachers can shout
And teachers can stare.
Teachers can help
And teachers can care.

Miles Rowbottom (7)
Exminster Primary School, Exeter

My Drawer

In my drawer I keep . . .
One furry rabbit
Two gigantic, cuddly penguins
Three Star Wars ships
Four bulging bags of money
Five Tamagotchi Version 4s
Six photograph albums
Seven packs of sweets
Eight odd socks
Nine chests of gold
Ten big balls of dust.

Samuel Hallett (8)
Exminster Primary School, Exeter

Teachers Can . . .

Teachers can teach
And teachers can talk.

Teachers can eat
And teachers can walk.

Teachers can shout
And teachers bake.

Teachers can play
And teachers can make.

Hazel McCorriston (7)
Exminster Primary School, Exeter

Winter

It was December
Cold and frosty
The sun through the clouds was shining
Snow lay softly on the ground
Crunching when I walked through.

I could hear the laughter of children
In the distance
Still walking with my head down
I went on
Coming to a glistening, gleaming lake.

I could see it tangled
In fishermen's line
This greeny-yellow duck
I couldn't decide whether to help or not
I pulled him out, but it was too late.

I ran home to get help
But when I got back
I had been too long.

In my sleep I see him,
    Quacking with his friends
        But I know he is safe now!

Ellie Stone (9)
Grenville College, Bideford

Mornings In Winter

When the grass is stiff and cold
I make footprints and snowmen
When the whistling wind blows cold leaves
I go travelling down a tiny hill on my sledge
Mornings in winter
When I am freezing cold
I curl up near the fire
When I am so bored
I run around the garden.

Joey Klymow (9)
Grenville College, Bideford

Winter

Snowing
heavily on the little village.
Many cheerful, cosy, contented
children outside playing joyfully
having fun making snowmen!

Ice skating
friends together on a frozen pond.
Laughing merrily together as they
glide across the lake!

Reindeer
galloping through woods
on Christmas night
sky so black,
stars so bright!

Araminta Pain (10)
Grenville College, Bideford

Happiness

Happiness is a wonderful yellow glow like a beautiful sun
who stands like a giant against the blue sky.
Happiness is the gentle sound of a sweet summer's day,
with wind whistling in the trees
and the exciting echo of children's laughter.
Happiness is like the smell of wondrous perfume,
made with jasmine and daisies, by the gentle hand of Venus.
Happiness is like a tropical sun, setting on a crystal-blue sea,
always gleaming back as it floats away.
Happiness reminds me of a beautiful cat with fur as soft as silk,
with a glimmering crystal collar.

Cassandra Allis (11)
Holymead Junior School, Bristol

Love

Love is pink like a giant piece of candyfloss waiting to be eaten.
Love looks like a massive, puffy cloud, hovering over the world.
Love smells like a blossoming flower, opening up
and sniffing the morning breeze.
Love sounds like a tweeting bird, spreading her magnificent wings.
Love is like bubblegum, sweet, tasting of wonderful delight.
Love is like a satin cushion, rubbing softly on your skin.
Love reminds me of my friends.

Natasha Blundal (11)
Holymead Junior School, Bristol

Ecstatic

Ecstatic is yellow like a bright, glistening sun beaming down on us.
Ecstatic is like a drum beating at a dramatic, fast pace,
then hitting a golden cymbal.
Ecstatic is like a sweet, strong smell of angels' perfume.
Ecstatic is like a big, sugary candy cane, reflecting the deep,
blue ocean.
Ecstatic is like a sunset laughing above an emerald-green hill.

Amber Turner-Williams (10)
Holymead Junior School, Bristol

Happiness

Happiness is yellow like a glowing, gleaming sun.
Happiness is like a flute being blown very quietly.
Happiness is like the sweet smell of flowers waiting to be picked.
Happiness is like a brand new car sparkling in the sunlight.
Happiness is my bright birthday balloons hanging on the wall.
Happiness reminds me of my family laughing happily.

Amy Wootton (11)
Holymead Junior School, Bristol

Excitement

Excitement is like a gleaming, glowing sunbeam.
Excitement is like a dramatic, fast-paced orchestra.
Excitement is like the sweet smell of chocolate chip cookies
                          on a freezing winter's eve.
Excitement is like a forbidden land over a high hill,
                          with candy trees and sugary grass.
Excitement is like the happy time of fluttery, glittery, friendly fairies
                          at my 4th birthday.

Bethany Pullen (10)
Holymead Junior School, Bristol

Disappointed

Disappointed is black like when you unwrap a perfect present
with nothing inside except brown cardboard.
Disappointed is like a teardrop falling slowly to the ground.
Disappointed is like a rotten, ugly flower,
just sitting on the window seat.
Disappointed is like a ball of bad air floating around in the sky.
Disappointed is like a memory of your hidden past.

Alisha Robinson (11)
Holymead Junior School, Bristol

Happiness

Happiness is green like a field of trees.
Happiness is like a chorus of laughter.
Happiness is like a sweet bed of flowers.
Happiness is like a comfy armchair, in front of the fire.
Happiness is like a big present, opened on Christmas Day.

Hannah Larkins (11)
Holymead Junior School, Bristol

Happiness

Happiness is yellow like a golden sun,
beaming and gleaming in your eyes.
Happiness is like a bunch of children,
giggling happily in a field of flowers.
Happiness is like a crumbly cupcake,
with a scent of daisies on the side.
Happiness is like a bundle of children,
playing a game with their cheerful friends.
Happiness is like an angel,
floating down from Heaven.

Kayleigh Amott (11)
Holymead Junior School, Bristol

Love

Love is red like blossoming roses all over the garden.
Love is a snow-white angel, plucking your heartstrings.
Love is like a golden pasty, cooling on the table.
Love is like a dream come down from Heaven.
This feeling reminds me of a green forest,
breaking through the ice-cold blanket of snow,
on a cold winter's day.

Beth Holland (11)
Holymead Junior School, Bristol

Love

Love is like lovely pink and white roses, falling in the garden.
Love is like a singing, quiet choir.
Love is like a fresh-born rose.
Love is like a little pig, floating in the air.
Love is like butter melting in your hands.
It reminds me of my best dog, Rosie.

Amelia Hasell (10)
Holymead Junior School, Bristol

Cheerful

Cheerful is yellow like the bright, happy sun,
spreading his spell over us all.
Cheerful is like butterflies, fluttering their beautiful,
graceful wings around my head.
Cheerful is like a sweet, fruity scent from a rose,
growing from a bud into a flower.
Cheerful is like a rose petal being held and never letting go.
Cheerful is like a baby giggling for the very first time.

Georgia Edmonds (10)
Holymead Junior School, Bristol

Love

Love is pink like a fluttering butterfly in the glistening sun.
Love is a pure white angel singing in the crystal-blue sky.
Love is like the golden rose blossoming in the sunset.
Love is a dream, made in Heaven.
Love is like a white fluffy cloud,
floating down to Earth to take me to Heaven.

Ella Griffiths (11)
Holymead Junior School, Bristol

Disappointment

Disappointment is grey like a bored sky waiting for good weather.
Disappointment is a ting on a triangle wanting more sound.
Disappointment is a faint smell of custard losing its taste.
Disappointment is a cloud bursting out all its tears.
Disappointment is like a split-up parent, always letting you down.

Shannon Darby-Jones (10)
Holymead Junior School, Bristol

Red

Red is everywhere, it's angry,
like a boiling soup, bubbling to and fro.
It sounds like a person yelling in pain.
It looks like a scorching sun,
exploding around the world.
It's like a sour chewy,
popping out of its wrapper into the mouth.
It reminds me of a big ball
going around a football pitch.

Lily Burt (10)
Holymead Junior School, Bristol

Hungry

Hungry is green like meadows of grass
Hungry is like butterflies flying in my stomach
Hungry is like a cooked dinner roasting in the oven
Hungry is like a kitten groaning in pain
Hungry reminds me of the memories of the past.

Jessica Barter (11)
Holymead Junior School, Bristol

Happiness

Happiness is yellow like a sunbeam.
Happiness is like a giggle.
Happiness is the sweet smell of perfume.
Happiness is a lovely hot day on the beach.
Happiness is the taste of a sweet apple.

Joel Rowbottom (11)
Holymead Junior School, Bristol

Love

Love is like a pink paintbrush, running along a fresh piece of paper.
Love is like a harp being played by angels.
Love is like a rare, strong perfume made in Heaven.
Love is like fluffy clouds, floating in the sky.
Love is my warm bed.

It reminds me of home.

Adam Broadbent (10)
Holymead Junior School, Bristol

Blue As Sadness

Sadness is like a tear falling from your eye.
Sadness sounds like a bottle smashing on the floor.
Sadness smells like lava pouring out from a volcano.
Sadness looks like someone stealing my lucky charm.
Sadness reminds me of my nan,
who I never met, dying.

Chelsie Roberts (11)
Holymead Junior School, Bristol

Love

Love is a pink flirty salsa flamingo.
Love is like a harp playing happily, while you take the special moment.
Love is like a box of chocolates being cast by a spell.
Love is a cute cupid, playing in the air.
Love is like a memory of your very first kiss.

Tilly Bryant (11)
Holymead Junior School, Bristol

Cheerful

Cheerful is yellow like the bright beaming sun,
shining over us all, warming us thoroughly and making us smile.

Cheerful is like the beautiful singing birds, tweeting at me happily, filling
my ears with their lovely sound through all the seasons.

Cheerful is like the sweet-smelling sunflower pollen, drifting through the
sky, bringing a fresh fragrance flowing past my nose.

Cheerful is like a pretty yellow rose, being picked up and admired by
everyone, from everywhere around, bringing happiness and
joy to them.

It tastes like mouth-watering fruits, their juice oozing into my mouth and
running down the back of my throat, filling me with satisfaction.

It reminds me of memorable days with my glorious family, at the sandy
beach and the crystal clear sea, but most of all the glittering scorching
sun and being with my family.

And that's the features of cheerfulness!

Emily Putnam (11)
Holymead Junior School, Bristol

Calm

Calm is blue like a river, running down.
Calm sounds like tweeting birds in the morning.
Calm reminds me of relaxing and seeing the clouds go by.
Calm smells like flowers picked fresh.
Calm is like a beautiful butterfly, opening its wings and taking flight.

Alison Payne (11)
Holymead Junior School, Bristol

If I Were . . .

If I were an animal I'd surely have to be
The largest thing you can possibly imagine,
And elephant, that's me!

If I were a racing car I'd surely have to be
Speedy, speedy round the track,
A Ferrari I would be!

If I were an insect I'd surely have to be
1 step, 2 steps,
A stick insect on a tree!

If I were a vegetable I'd surely have to be
A tiny, little green ball,
A pea, just for me!

But I don't want to be any of these things,
No I really don't want to be,
Because I'm really happy just in being
Me!

Sam Stevenson (10)
St Breock Primary School, Wadebridge

By The Sea

Hear the rocks bashing,
Hear the waves roar,
Hear the shells clanking
By the seashore.

See the sun shining,
See the rippled sand floor,
See the grass blowing
By the seashore.

Jo Temple (9)
St Breock Primary School, Wadebridge

I Would Love To Be . . .

I would love to be a bird
I could fly over the sea
I would love to be a bird
A bird I could be
I could fly up high
I could dive down low
I could fly wherever
I want to go!

I would love to be a rabbit
I could run so very fast
I would love to be a rabbit
I could run through tickly grass
I could jump up high
I could dig down low
I could bounce wherever
I want to go!

It's the end of the day
Now I see
All I want to be . . .
Is me!

Tegan Benney (10)
St Breock Primary School, Wadebridge

My Rabbit Heather

I love my pet Heather
And I'll love her forever
I love her cute paws
And her very sharp claws!

She loves it when I feed her
So I think that you should know
We'll love each other to the end
Because I'm truly her
Best friend!

India Laing (9)
St Breock Primary School, Wadebridge

Animals

Ten tiny, tiptoeing turtles
Nine naughty, noisy newts
Eight ever-eating elephants
Seven snoozing, snoring snakes
Six slimy, squashy slugs
Five furry, fat foxes
Four fiddling, frustrated frogs
Three thinking, thoughtful thrushes
Two teasing, troublesome tigers
One ordinary, organised ox.

Ella Wall (10)
St Breock Primary School, Wadebridge

Colour

Colour, colour all around,
It makes you feel fuzzy,
It's a lovely feeling,
Pink feels fluffy,
Red feels like anger,
Blue feels calm,
Green feels cosy,
Black feels like darkness,
Purple feels like secrets,
Those are the colours.

Rhys Jones (8)
St Breock Primary School, Wadebridge

Me

Clever and delightful,
Sporty, lovely and brainy,
Best at everything,
That's me.
(But perhaps not very modest!)

Toby Tinker (8)
St Breock Primary School, Wadebridge

Paddle, Paddle, Paddle, Spring

Paddle, paddle, paddle, spring
If I catch the wave?
Paddle, paddle, paddle, spring
Could I carve the left?
Paddle, paddle, paddle, spring
Can I carve the right?
Paddle, paddle, paddle, spring
A surge of speed
Paddle, paddle, paddle, spring
A tube building from behind
Paddle, paddle, paddle, spring up!
Surfing's what I do!

Laura Vinton (10)
St Breock Primary School, Wadebridge

Me And Jess

Me and Jess are just good friends,
We play together and it never ends.
We like to dance, it's so much fun,
We once even made a bun!
Wherever we go there's no mess,
Just me and Jess!

Lauren Dennis (10)
St Breock Primary School, Wadebridge

My Thoughts

If my happy thoughts took shape,
they would be like a gleaming, shining sun,
warming up the Earth with colourful glitter.

If my terrible thoughts took shape,
they would be like a terrifying tornado,
ripping me off the ground with everything coming up with me!

Joseph Williams (11)
St Mark's CE Primary School, Bude

Shark

Neither legs nor hands have I,
But I swim with fins,
And I seek
Blood, blood, blood!

Neither ears nor helmets have I,
But I bite with razor-sharp teeth,
And I sense
Blood, blood, blood!

I master every movement
For I swim proudly and silently,
And I taste
Blood, blood, blood!

Ben Pengilly (10)
St Mark's CE Primary School, Bude

The Wildcat Song

Neither guns nor missiles have I,
But I have claws and sharp teeth,
And I can
Scratch, scratch, scratch!

Neither bows nor swords have I,
But I can spit, yowl and scrape,
And I can
Scratch, scratch, scratch!

I master every movement,
For I leap, run and prowl,
And I can
Scratch, scratch, scratch!

Catalina Gutierrez (8)
St Mark's CE Primary School, Bude

Weather

If my peaceful thoughts took shape,
they would be like sunshine rising up in the sky,
casting its rays across the world.

If my frustrated thoughts took shape,
they would be like a tornado ripping through a town,
destroying everything in its path.

If my sad thoughts took shape,
they would be like black clouds covering over the sun,
casting shadows on the ground.

If my bored thoughts took shape,
they would be like drizzle making the ground wet and muddy,
so no one could go outside.

Holly McLellan (11)
St Mark's CE Primary School, Bude

Weather

If my furious thoughts took shape,
it would be like lightning striking the ground.

If my happy thoughts took shape,
it would be like the sun rising on a frosty morning.

If my sad thoughts took shape,
it would be like the breeze brushing my face.

If my terrified thoughts took shape,
it would be like thunder crashing on the ocean wide.

Jack Savage (8)
St Mark's CE Primary School, Bude

Weather

If my scared thoughts took shape,
they would be like clouds covering the light blue, clear sky.

If my frustrated thoughts took shape,
they would be like a hurricane
destroying all the blue and green world.

If my bored thoughts took shape,
they would be like a blanket of fog covering the sky in its path.

If my angry thoughts took shape,
they would be like a tornado, sucking up the sea
and puking it back up.

Fay Mannix (10)
St Mark's CE Primary School, Bude

Weather

If my cheerful thoughts took shape,
they would be like fluffy snow drifting gracefully through the sky.

If my bored thoughts took shape,
they would be like never-ending fog, gripping tightly to the world.

If my lonely thoughts took shape,
they would be like stone-cold frost blocking me out.

If my peaceful thoughts took shape,
they would be like a gentle breeze, drifting through my hair.

Emelye Davies (11)
St Mark's CE Primary School, Bude

Thoughts

If my loving thoughts took shape,
they would be like a beautiful sunny day in the middle of August
with children playing everywhere.

If my sad thoughts took shape,
they would be like murderous rain falling everywhere.

If my frustrated thoughts took shape,
they would be like a red-hot flame burning its life away.

If my unhappy thoughts took shape,
they would be like an eclipse blocking out the sun.

Kitty Harding (10)
St Mark's CE Primary School, Bude

The Weather

If my angry thoughts took shape,
they would be like thunder booming to its heart's content.

If my furious thoughts took shape,
they would be like a typhoon-torn sea, crashing against the cliff.

If my happy thoughts took shape,
they would be like the sun beaming on the gleaming sea.

If my cheerful thoughts took shape,
they would be like snow dancing through the trees.

Aiden Gill (9)
St Mark's CE Primary School, Bude

Weather

If my happy thoughts took shape,
they would be like dew on a spring morning.

If my angry thoughts took shape,
they would be like a hurricane destroying and ruining America.

If my cheerful thoughts took shape,
they would be like snow coming slowly down
and settling on the grass.

If my miserable thoughts took shape,
they would be like hail hitting the floor, striking my face.

Amy Hands (11)
St Mark's CE Primary School, Bude

Weather

If my happy thoughts took shape,
they would be like the sun shining over the sea.

If my angry thoughts took shape,
they would be like a twister, crushing the land.

If my cheerful thoughts took shape,
they would be like snow dancing in the air.

If my unhappy thoughts took shape,
they would be like the drizzling rain falling.

Emma Hands (11)
St Mark's CE Primary School, Bude

The Tiger Song

Neither daggers nor knives have I
But I have sharp, stabbing claws,
And I have
Stripes, stripes, stripes!

Neither horns nor hooves have I
But I have amazing, powerful teeth,
And I can
Eat, eat, eat!

I master every movement
For I am sly and quiet,
And I am
Silent, silent, silent!

Eleanor Townsend (9)
St Mark's CE Primary School, Bude

Animal Poem

Snake.
Brighter
Than the warm, summer sun
Slithers through the grass
Eyes like
Red rubies
Scanning the fields.
He slowly bends
His neck back and
Strikes!

Ciaran Tape (10)
St Mark's CE Primary School, Bude

The Chameleon Song

Neither army nor helmet have I
But I have weapons of disguise
And I have
Colour, colour, colour!

Neither grappling hook or rope have I
But I have suckers on my fingertips
And I have
Colour, colour, colour!

I master every movement
For I scamper, scurry and sprint
And I have
Colour, colour, colour!

Toby Miles (8)
St Mark's CE Primary School, Bude

Eagle

Eagle,
Faster
Than light.
Searching the field,
Like a bomb ready to drop.
Talons as sharp as razors,
Eyes hard as marbles.
Seeking, fixing
On to its prey.

Ben Pye (10)
St Mark's CE Primary School, Bude

Cheetah Song

Neither guns nor missiles have I,
But I am silent and sly,
And I can run to
Catch, catch, catch!

Neither engine nor turbo have I,
But I am fast and fearsome,
And I spring to
Catch, catch, catch!

I master every movement,
For I lock on to my prey,
And I pounce to
Kill, kill, kill!

Charlotte Whitfield (8)
St Mark's CE Primary School, Bude

Weather

If my happy thoughts took shape
they would be like the sun shining
Like a star at night.

If my bored thoughts took shape
They would be like the fog blocking
Everybody's view.

If my excited thoughts took shape
They would be like twinkling snowflakes
Flying to the grass.

Demie Williams-Green (9)
St Mark's CE Primary School, Bude

The Shark Song

Neither legs nor arms have I,
But I swim, hunt, eat, sleep.
And I
Bite, bite, bite!

Neither breath nor cry have I,
I fight with my teeth,
And I
Bite, bite, bite!

I master every movement,
Swim, kill, and eat,
And I bite, bite, bite!

Reuben Farrell (10)
St Mark's CE Primary School, Bude

Kestrel

Kestrel,
Silently,
Soaring through the sky.
Searching the ground,
Till suddenly he finds
And fixes his gaze,
He hovers . . .
Then without warning
Drops.
Plummeting,
Seizing, snatching,
Snapping at his prey.
Then silence.

Winnie Stubbs (9)
St Mark's CE Primary School, Bude

Weather

If my furious thoughts took shape,
they would be like a twister destroying a farm in America.

If my cheerful thoughts took shape,
they would be like snow settling and making a big white sail.

If my petrified thoughts took shape,
they would be like a blizzard swarming over the ice.

If my miserable thoughts took shape,
they would be like fog, butchering the light.

William Phipps (10)
St Mark's CE Primary School, Bude

Lion

A tangled mass of gold,
Like a royal crown.
Crouching and creeping,
Camouflaged in swaying grass.
Proudly prowling,
Hunting for prey,
Or the swish of a tail,
Lazily, lying in the sun.

Charlotte Chapman (10)
St Mark's CE Primary School, Bude

Dolphin

Dolphin
An acrobat,
Diving through a hoop.
A splashing swimmer.
A gymnast
With sleek, shining leotard,
Yet fins
As sharp as glass.

Marisa Taylor (10)
St Mark's CE Primary School, Bude

What Is A Cheetah?

A cheetah is a rocket
On its way to Mars.

It is a golden streak
That covers the outback
The same colour
As the stars.

Lucy Perry (10)
St Mark's CE Primary School, Bude

Cowboy Cactus

If
I was
not a
cactus I
would be a cowboy
counting down to six
1 click of the gun
2 men being hanged
3 men having a stand off
4 men in the mud having a fight
5 men stealing from a girl
6 men riding in the sunset, home.

Harrison Raymont (10)
St Mary's CE School, Truro

My Imaginary Monster

My imaginary monster has 105 teeth,
Some are shaped like cones but some are chipped,
He has arms like lines.
4 arms, gosh, what a lot.
Two terrible legs that have spots on the knees.
But I have one more thing to say . . .
I am that monster!

Leah Richards (9)
St Mary's CE School, Truro

I Wonder

I do wonder what is behind the teacher's desk.
Maybe one elephant,
And two rats, nibbling on cheese,
Maybe three cats,
And four dogs to fight,
Maybe five horses,
And six gorillas to shout,
Maybe seven fish
And eight bowls of water to put the fish in.
But is that really possible?

Emily Parsons (10)
St Mary's CE School, Truro

If I Were A Shape

I would be a sphere . . .
I would be a bowling ball going for strike.
I would be a football going for goal.
I would be a basketball going into the net.
I would be a basketball going to the next person.
I would be a golf ball going into the hole.
I would be a ping-pong ball being hit against the table.
If I could be a shape
I would be a star . . .
I would be Jonny Wilkinson going for the try.

James Doyle (10)
St Mary's CE School, Truro

If I Were A Shape

If I were a shape I'd be a triangle.
If I were a snooker ball holder I'd be a triangle.
If I were a pyramid I would be high.
If I were a roof on the home I'd keep my family dry.

Nathan Smith (9)
St Mary's CE School, Truro

10 Snoring Teachers

10 snoring teachers lying on the floor,
one woke up and left because the others were a bore.

9 snoring teachers standing by the gate,
one woke up and went away because she didn't have a mate.

8 snoring teachers sitting on the wall,
one woke up and went away to go shopping at the mall.

7 snoring teachers sitting on a chair,
one woke up and went away to her secret lair.

6 snoring teachers sitting on a bench,
one woke up and went off to get his wrench.

5 snoring teachers sitting on a table,
one woke up and went away to see her horse in the stable.

4 snoring teachers lying in the vent,
one woke up to find that the vent was now bent.

3 snoring teachers lying on a float,
one woke up and fell in the moat.

2 snoring teachers sitting on the grass,
one woke up to play his trumpet made of brass.

1 snoring teacher eating a bun,
she woke up and ran away.
So then there were none!

Molly Mason (9)
St Mary's CE School, Truro

Maths Pudding

A cup of 5 times tables
A lot of shapes
A pinch of 1 divided by 1
A drop of 20 plus 20
A jug of 100 times 100
And eat.

Fleur Anderson (9)
St Mary's CE School, Truro

If I Were A Shape

If I were a shape
I'd be a triangle.
I'd be part of the Eiffel Tower, shining in the sun.
I'd be a point of a star, up in the sky.
I'd be a side of a pyramid, way over in Egypt.
If only I were a triangle . . .

If I were a square
I'd be the screen of a plasma TV.
I'd be a sandwich that could never be swallowed.
I'd be a speaker of a DJ set.
If only I were a square . .

If I were a star
I'd be Björn Ulvaeus.

Aaron Wilton (10)
St Mary's CE School, Truro

Counting Scary Numbers

One scary number eating roasted leg
Two scary numbers drinking blood
Three scary numbers eating three legs
Four scary numbers cooking four hands
Five scary numbers finding our weakness
Six scary numbers killing humans
Seven scary numbers eating brain gum
Eight scary numbers eating heads
Nine scary numbers having a rest.
Ten scary numbers being killed by a monster.

Alex Cotton (9)
St Mary's CE School, Truro

Revolting Rubbish Rhyme

I was walking in the countryside,
When I smelt the horrible smell, I had to hide.
The closer I got the smell got stronger,
And I didn't want to stay much longer.
I ran back down the muddy path,
I really wanted to get in the bath,
The smell of rubbish faded away,
It was rotting apples there that day.
Don't drop rubbish on the ground,
Find a bin and
Put it in!

Megan Watkinson (10)
The Maynard School, Exeter

Who Is This Man?

Here comes a knight in his polished armour.
Here comes a knight striding to his horse.
Here comes a knight buckling up his steed.
       Who is this man?

This brave knight has his sword and shield.
This brave knight is riding to battle.
This brave knight is willing to fight.
       Who is this man?

His shield and dagger such a sight to see.
His shield and dagger shine in the sun.
His shield and dagger protect him well.
       Who is this man?

I know this man he must be King Arthur.
I know him well for I am his knight.
I know this man, oh yes, I know him!
       It must be him!

Millie Prichard (9)
Urchfont CE Primary School, Nr Devizes

Knight

I see a knight in shining armour.
I see a knight so able and brave.
I see a knight ready for battle,
with his old and trusty steed.

His sword is long and made of steel.
His shield protects him from any foe.
His helmet covers his neck,
A plate covers his big chest.

His mother and father have long since died.
When death struck Merlin took him to Kay,
He was so sad that he ran away to Merlin in the forest.

He pulled the magic sword from the stone.
Afterwards he was crowned the high king.
And his wizard friend called Merlin,
Brought him Bercelet, a friend.

Patrick Lee (7)
Urchfont CE Primary School, Nr Devizes

Excalibur

The shining jewelled Excalibur
Given by Merlin to Arthur
As son of the high king, Uthur.

Excalibur is held in hand
A white and gleaming hand
The hand is like gleaming white sand.

The hand in the lake is shaking
Excalibur is waking up
At home Arthur's hand is waking.

Charlotte Kinnaird (8)
Urchfont CE Primary School, Nr Devizes

Start To Heart

Merlin goes to Uther King.
Takes him to Tintagel dim.
Then he meets their queen, Igraine.
Merlin casts a spell in vain.

'Tis a boy this newborn babe.
Arthur High shall be his name.
When he grows he shall be king.
Peace through lands shall be his thing.

He pulls the sword out of the stone.
He will sit proudly on the throne.
He's crowned high king that boy of twelve.
Released the sword so deeply delved.

He'll make court at Camelot.
With knights such as Lancelot.
At a round table he'll sit.
Knights around him brave and fit.

He rides to battle on his horse.
To drive the Saxons off their course.
Bloodshed, killing, coloured grass red.
Now high king Arthur pleads for bed.

There's a girl though the window.
On her harmonic cello.
Making beautiful music.
Her sweet name is Guinevere.

Annabel Lee (8)
Urchfont CE Primary School, Nr Devizes

Arthur's World

Arthur's world surrounded by foes.
Arthur's world is a great place.
Arthur's world has heavy blows.
Arthur's world.

Arthur's land as the sea.
Arthur's land great to be seen.
Arthur's land no sign of glee.
Arthur's land.

Arthur's wife will always be here.
Arthur's wife hopeful of glee.
Arthur's wife great Guinevere.
Arthur's wife.

Arthur's knights have a tasty meal.
Arthur's knights as strong as steel.
Arthur's knights can always feel.
Arthur's knights.

Arthur's Camelot shining bright.
Arthur's Camelot strong with might.
Arthur's Camelot at night.
Arthur's Camelot.

Arthur's world surrounded by friends.
Arthur's world great land again.
Arthur's world up with the trends.
Arthur's world.

Martin Coombes (9)
Urchfont CE Primary School, Nr Devizes

I See A Knight

I see a brave knight,
In shining metal armour.
With a sword so bright,
He doesn't have a father.

I see a brave knight,
Getting ready for battle.
Battling in the night,
It made his armour rattle.

I see a brave knight,
Fighting for life and glory.
He has had a fight,
The battlefield is gory.

Jamie Hall (8)
Urchfont CE Primary School, Nr Devizes

King Arthur

King Arthur is a knight.
What a sight to see him fight,
Because King Arthur is a knight.

Merlin is a wizard.
In his spells he uses lizards,
Because Merlin is a wizard.

Guinevere is a wife.
What a golden sight,
Because Guinevere is a wife.

Camelot is Arthur's home.
Surrounded by marshy land,
Because Camelot is a home.

William Everett (8)
Urchfont CE Primary School, Nr Devizes

Armour

The brave knight was fierce
And he was strong and had shining armour
He had a strong horse that was scraping
His hooves on the floor angrily.

The horse charges and the knight raises
His big, silver sword
His armour is his silver body shield
And it protects him from his enemies' blows.

He walks through the wood, his armour glistening
And puts Guinevere on his big grey horse
And rides off to Tintagel castle
Where Igraine is waiting.

Amber Holloway (7)
Urchfont CE Primary School, Nr Devizes

King Arthur

Long ago a knight once stood
He lived in a castle called Camelot.
One night he had a lot to drink
And he saw a lady dressed in pink.
Her skin was as white as a sheet
And her hair was so soft and sweet.

Merlin was a famous wizard
He was a very nice wizard
He had a wand and topping it was a headless lizard.
He kept a good eye on Arthur
And looked after him very well.

Rosemary Vaux Murray (8)
Urchfont CE Primary School, Nr Devizes

King Arthur

Merlin went to the castle,
Where he met the great Lancelot.
Uther the king came with him,
To take him to Tintagel dim.
To take him to Igraine,

They had a newborn boy named Arthur.
Through the great land he was to maintain
Lots of peace and love to reign again.
He grew up to be a great king

Arthur saw the great stone,
On the top perched a robin
To try and guide him to the stone,
He grasped the sword quite tightly,
Then tried to pull it out.

Many a knight had tried too,
To pull it out with strength and might,
They couldn't do it,
So they left it in the granite stone.

But the boy
Quickly got it out,
All alone
In the dark courtyard.

But Sir Kay lied to Sir Egbert,
Telling him that he would be king,
But he didn't believe him,
Because that was all he wanted.
When Arthur got much older,
He went to a huge round table.
He had a wonderful feast,

Then he met the beautiful Guinevere
She was nice,
She was quite pretty,
Blonde long hair
Blowing in the wind.

They got married in a church,
A shiny long dress worn by her.
What a beautiful place here.
Arthur battled Pelanore,
He realised he was now king,
He went to the lake, Avalon
And from the Lady of the Lake
He got a new, shining sword.

Ellie Gibbs (9)
Urchfont CE Primary School, Nr Devizes

King Arthur

King Arthur was a legend who lived long ago.
With his sword called Excalibur he fought every foe.
His knights were all brave and his table was round.
Camelot his castle he built on high ground.

Sir Lancelot sat at Arthur's right hand,
And Merlin the wizard was part of the band.
The stone held the sword that no one could shift,
But Arthur was chosen to give it a lift.

Maddy Borrill (8)
Urchfont CE Primary School, Nr Devizes

A Knight

A knight charges into battle on his grey horse.
It is a champion course.
Off he goes up the hill,
Determined to kill.

He fights with all his might,
Dead knights, what a sight!
Ching-ching go the swords
As the red blood pours.

Thomas Middleton (7)
Urchfont CE Primary School, Nr Devizes

The Legend Of King Arthur

In the misty marshes lie,
Reaching to the cloudless sky,
Camelot, in marshes green,
Dimming light glow can be seen.

In this castle lives a king,
Young is he, with peace to bring,
At a table, knights sit here,
With queen to be, Guinevere.

Merlin sits there with the knights,
Telling tales of dragon fights,
Arthur then bursts in to say,
'We must go and fight away'.

So off they rode to battle,
And made their armour rattle,
Need to battle with a king,
Then, later a marv'lous thing.

He battled well to start with,
It broke the sword he fought with,
Then, at last, the moment came,
Bercelet's moment of fame.

Had to get another sword,
Couldn't fight, he would be bored,
So he went with Merlin to
Where he could get a sword new.

Merlin goes and dances on,
Till they get to Avalon,
Then the waves begin to shake,
A figure rises out the lake.

He rowed towards the figure,
And grasped the sword with vigour,
He pulled it out of the hand,
And headed back to the land.

Then he married Guinevere,
Took her to Camelot dear,
There they had a great big feast,
It was the night of the east.

Then the figure came to see,
If Merlin loved her, if he
Comes with her and is happy,
Everyone lives happily.

Lorna Frankel (8)
Urchfont CE Primary School, Nr Devizes

Excalibur The Sword

With jewels on its handle and a blade of steel,
Any who come near to it are forced to kneel.
As protection against the forces of darkness.

Arthur is kept out of harm by its sharpness.
On his arm a shield of steel and of England.
The shining Excalibur held in his hand.

Scott Livermore (8)
Urchfont CE Primary School, Nr Devizes

Excalibur

She was ghostlike as she came out of the lake.
In her hand a silver sword she had made.
Across the still waters she glided along
To give Arthur the sharp sword.
With the sword in his hand he mounted his horse
And rode to Camelot at full force.

Amber Weyman (7)
Urchfont CE Primary School, Nr Devizes

King Arthur

King Arthur
King Arthur is a knight
He has a round table
They do lots of fighting.

Merlin
Merlin is a wizard
He likes to use lizards
He has a starry hat

Guinevere

Guinevere plays a harp
Guinevere plays sharp.

Thomas Honeychurch (7)
Urchfont CE Primary School, Nr Devizes

My Mum

My mum is so cool
She never does act like a fool
My mum is simply the best
She is better than all the rest
She is a great and wicked nan
But sadly there is really no man
Well that's my mum
Now it's time to have some fun.

Sarah Horswell (11)
Widey Court Primary School, Plymouth

Young Writers Information

We hope you have enjoyed reading this book - and that you will continue to enjoy it in the coming years.

If you like reading and writing poetry drop us a line, or give us a call, and we'll send you a free information pack.

Alternatively if you would like to order further copies of this book or any of our other titles, then please give us a call or log onto our website at www.youngwriters.co.uk

Young Writers Information
Remus House
Coltsfoot Drive
Peterborough
PE2 9JX

(01733) 890066